Prepare For Tests at Interview

for

Graduates and Managers

Prepare for
tests at interview
for graduates & managers

Robert Williams

Published by the NFER-NELSON Publishing Company Ltd, Darville House,
2 Oxford Road East, Windsor, Berkshire SL4 1DF, UK.

Copyright © NFER-NELSON, 1999.

ISBN 0 7005 1601 8

Typesetting and design by Francis Design.

Printed in Great Britain.

Code 0090007635

1(10.99)

Contents

Acknowledgements

The author expresses his thanks to the following people for their valuable contributions:

Helen Bradley, Ian Florance, Scarlet Leatham, Louise Oxley, Fiona Penn, Anne Marie Ryan, Jackie Scullard, Kim Stephenson and JP Westwood.

Chapter 1

Introduction

What is a psychometric assessment?

Today's graduates and managers at all levels are very likely to encounter one or more psychometric assessments at some stage when applying for jobs. Most medium to large-sized organisations recruiting graduates and managerial candidates now use psychometric assessments on a routine basis as part of their selection process. It is therefore essential for those undergoing a recruitment process to understand what a psychometric assessment is, how such assessments work, and how they can achieve their best possible performance.

While psychometric assessments are increasingly used in recruitment, they still form only one part of the selection process and have not replaced other selection methods. As we all know, not everyone is good at completing application forms or taking interviews. Psychometric assessments are a measurement device used by employers to gain a better understanding of an individual. In contrast to CVs or application forms a psychometric assessment offers an objective assessment of the abilities and aptitudes that an individual has and their potential for acquiring specific skills.

Unlike academic exams, psychometric assessments cannot be interpreted as a pass or fail on the basis of a single grade. As part of the development process of a psychometric assessment, it is taken by a large group of people who then serve as the standard comparison group for individuals taking the assessment in the future. The advantage of using standardised ability tests within a selection context is that they provide an additional means of comparing candidates to their academic attainment.

In addition to their use in graduate recruitment, psychometric assessments are used in selection right across the board, from unskilled work to managerial positions. Psychometric assessments also have a wide range of applications within an occupational setting, including counselling employees, assessing developmental needs and addressing teamworking issues. Commonly used in a guidance context by career counsellors, psychometric assessments help individuals to identify which of their skills match particular job demands.

How can *Prepare For* help me?

This book will not reveal how to pass psychometric assessments. Psychometric assessments are not pass or fail instruments. Instead this book aims to explain the various test formats in common use and allay any anxiety connected with psychometric assessments. By becoming familiar with these test formats, candidates will be better able to perform at their best on the selection day.

Working through ASE's practice questions should improve confidence about sitting selection tests and reduce anxiety about taking psychometric assessments. These practice questions aim to cover the wide range of psychometric assessments that graduates and managers from different disciplines may encounter. These range from well-known general ability and personality assessments to tests of specific abilities, such as verbal skills and numerical reasoning. Aiming to be truly comprehensive, this book devotes a chapter to each of the major types of psychometric assessment. Brief descriptions of each type of assessment featured are given at the start of each section, followed by an explanation of what each question type is assessing and a block of examples for the reader to try. Up-to-date information about preparation and advice on the best strategies to employ when taking a psychometric assessment is also provided. The assessments presented here are designed to be similar to those commonly encountered as part of a selection process.

ASE, like some of the other major test publishers, publishes Test User Guides which can be provided to help familiarise candidates. If one of these guides is not supplied prior to the test session, contact the company testing you in order to request one.

What type of assessments am I likely to be given?

A well-designed selection procedure focuses on predicting a person's competency within a particular work context. Psychometric assessments only form one part of the selection procedure and must be interpreted alongside other selection procedures and the candidate's background information. Another commonly used technique for selecting candidates at graduate or managerial level is the assessment centre, where ability and personality assessments are often used as part of an integrated package, which include job simulation exercises, interviews, written exercises, group discussions and role play.

The generic term ability tests is often used interchangeably with that of aptitude tests, when in fact the latter refers to a more specific assessment category. Aptitude tests measure the potential for reaching a particular ability level, whereas attainment or achievement tests aim to measure the ability level which has already been reached. A school maths exam will show the level of mathematical ability achieved by a student. A numerical reasoning test, such as those found in *Prepare For*, can be used to predict the potential an applicant has to apply their mathematical skills at work.

Ability tests may be divided into different sections with a set time limit for each section. Similarly, a graduate or managerial assessment may include more than one ability assessment: a verbal, a numerical and/or a non-verbal assessment. Individuals must also be prepared to take personality assessments. Personality assessments can give an indication of how well an individual applicant will fit into the existing workplace or team. Psychometric assessments can assess which applicants are most suited to the demands of the vacant job in terms of both ability and personality factors.

Isn't this just another exam?

Just as when sitting a school exam, the same questions and standardised instructions are given to everyone under timed conditions when taking a psychometric assessment. Psychometric assessments, however, place an even greater emphasis on standardisation than school exams, without giving any choice of the questions to be answered. This allows a trained test user to make comparisons between each individual's set of responses because everyone is subjected to the same set of conditions. Standardised test conditions are thus a vital part of ensuring that everyone is assessed in exactly the same manner. Precise administration instructions are provided by test publishers, such as ASE, enabling every test session to be conducted under the same standardised conditions. The standardised conditions extend to how each set of results is scored and interpreted – the overriding aim being to assess all candidates fairly.

How are the results interpreted?

After the assessment has been taken the total number of correct answers, known as the raw score, will be converted into a format which gives more meaning to it. A score without a frame of reference is meaningless and needs to be in a format that will allow it to be compared with other people's results. Each score is compared to those from a similar group of people, who have sat the same assessment on an earlier occasion. These representative groups are built up as part of the test development process and are often referred to as 'norm groups' or comparison groups.

To take an example, if someone scored on the 80th percentile, then this would mean that 80 per cent of the comparison population scored less than this. If this 80th percentile represented a graduate's performance on a verbal assessment, and the same graduate reached the 40th percentile on a numerical assessment, then a direct comparison can be made across the two assessments using the same comparison group. The important question can be answered: has the graduate demonstrated higher verbal or numerical ability, or are they both about the same?

After sitting a psychometric assessment as part of a selection process, the candidate should always receive some form of feedback on his or her performance. This is unlikely to be the actual raw score, although the feedback should include an adequate explanation of how the candidate performed relative to a particular comparison or norm group. It is particularly important for unsuccessful candidates to obtain feedback, which may take the form of a telephone discussion or a letter from the organisation concerned.

But is it reliable?

Reliability means that an assessment consistently provides accurate scores of the underlying ability or attainment being measured. This means that if a candidate sits a test on one occasion and then retakes the test soon afterwards (1 week – 3 months) their results on these two occasions should be fairly consistent.

But is it valid?

A psychometric assessment which has a high validity has been shown to adequately measure what it claims to measure. Actual data on how individuals perform on the job e.g. ratings, appraisal grades, are best for establishing an assessment's ability to predict success. Assessments may also be shown to predict, for example, the successful completion of a training course. Any measure of validity only applies to a particular work context. Thus, a mechanical reasoning assessment would be invalid for selecting jobs without any mechanical content.

But is it fair?

In order to be fair, a psychometric assessment should not discriminate in terms of ethnic origin, gender or disability. In other words, one particular group should not be more successful than another group in terms of a particular question or the assessment as a whole. Individual questions are tested for bias as part of the test development process in order to eliminate any that are unfair to either sex or to a particular ethnic minority group.

Chapter 2

The Assessment Day

Preparation

An invitation to attend a test session will provide details of where and when it will be held. In addition, it may include some practice questions or an explanation of why the particular assessments were chosen in the form of a test-taker's guide. The practice questions presented here should help put you in the right frame of mind.

Just as when taking other exams, an individual's performance will suffer from tiredness or illness. Always try to get plenty of sleep the night before. In the case of illness, ask to take the assessment at a later date. Individuals with restricted eyesight should let the organisation know in advance of the test session; Braille and large print versions are often available. People with hearing difficulties could easily be accommodated. If you have any special requirements it is important to let the organisation arranging the tests know in advance. The test administrator will be able to prepare any additional paperwork/facilities in advance in order for you to do your best on the day.

What to expect on the day

On the assessment day everyone will have received the same background information and will be provided with all the materials necessary to complete the assessment. These materials may include a calculator if it is deemed necessary, and scrap paper which will be collected in. On some tests calculators are not allowed but the test administrators will tell you this.

The administrator will read to you all the instructions which you will need to complete the assessment satisfactorily. When taking the assessment, it is very important to follow these instructions carefully. A couple of practice questions will probably be given before the testing session. Individuals who get these wrong or do not understand them should not worry, since the administrator will go through the answers to each of these. The aim is to ensure that everyone understands exactly what is expected, so it is very important to understand exactly how these answers were obtained. The administrator will be happy to answer any questions before the assessment starts, but he or she cannot answer questions about the content of the assessment or offer any assistance once the assessment has started.

The best strategies to use

- Try to keep as calm as possible in order to listen to all the instructions you are given.

- Don't skim read any of the instructions or any text at the start of each question. It is important that you are clear about how to answer the questions before starting.

- Practice questions are usually given at the start of any assessment. Use these as an opportunity to gain familiarity with the following: the format of both the questionnaire and the answer sheet, and how the answers should be marked on the answer sheet (using ticks, lines, crosses, circles etc.).

- In order to answer as many questions as possible in the limited time available, it is wise to adopt an appropriate strategy. This should be based on whether the test format presents a large number of questions in a short space of time or whether there will be a smaller number of more detailed questions to answer.

- Don't spend too long on a single question – remember that all questions are worth the same and the next question might be easier. If there is spare time at the end of the assessment, go back to any unanswered questions. Try to do as many questions as possible in the time allowed for the assessments, but do not worry if you do not finish.

- Check that the question number being completed always corresponds to the one given on the answer sheet. Be especially careful when coming to the end of a block of questions.

- When assessing difficult multiple-choice questions it may be useful to rule out one or two of the alternatives offered as being extremely unlikely to be correct.

- If you change an answer, make sure you mark the final answer clearly.

- If in doubt of an answer give the best estimate.

- In case of finishing early, go back and review your answers.

- Motivation is highly important, so try to keep a positive attitude throughout the assessment day.

How to take the practice questions

When taking the practice assessments, work through a whole set of examples and then consult the answers. For each example answered incorrectly, work through the question again until the answer is understood. This is a more effective form of learning, compared to simply finding out how many questions have been answered correctly.

No time limits are given for the practice questions presented here. It is up to the individual to set their own time limit or to simply work through each block at a steady pace.

Chapter 3

Introduction to Personality Questionnaires

The two main ways of measuring personality are the type and trait methods. A trait is defined as a specific piece of general behaviour that can characterise an individual, for example, being a perfectionist. The trait approach describes personality using a large number of scales by identifying which of an individual's traits are more characteristic when compared to other people. The type approach focuses on a smaller number of broad personality characteristics and emphasises an individual's preference for different types of behaviour.

There is no time limit for taking personality assessments, although some guidance will be provided on how long completing the test is likely to take. This will probably be between 15–40 minutes. Feedback from a personality test is split into a number of different personality types or traits. Within the context of personality testing, traits are frequently described using a number of dimensions.

Most personality questionnaires are designed to incorporate some means of establishing the honesty of the individual's responses overall. It is always best to try to be as honest as possible since these assessments are not looking for 'good' or 'bad' personalities.

Personality questionnaires

There follows examples of three different types of personality test, each with ten practice questions. The first set of ten questions relates to general behaviour. The second set of questions, starting at question number eleven, focuses specifically on behaviour at work. The third set of questions, numbered 21–30, asks the respondent to make a direct choice between the types of behaviour in which he or she usually engages. In the previous two sets of practice personality questions the answer options changed from question to question, whilst in the third set the answer chosen must be 'Yes', 'Sometimes' or 'No' for each question.

1) Do you often regret how you behaved towards someone?

   a) Yes
   b) Sometimes
   c) No

2) Have you ever found yourself checking the bill in a restaurant?

   a) Often
   b) Sometimes
   c) Never

3) Do you like to try new dishes?

   a) Often
   b) Sometimes
   c) Never

4) On holiday do you tend to spend more time on the beach than sightseeing?

   a) Usually
   b) About the same
   c) Never

5) When meeting people for the first time, do you find yourself doing most of the talking?

   a) Usually
   b) About the same
   c) Never

6) Do you try to offer help to friends who are encountering problems?

   a) Often
   b) Sometimes
   c) Never

7) Have you ever found yourself searching for lost bills or tickets?

   a) Often
   b) Sometimes
   c) Never

8) Do you always answer honestly when asked personal questions?

   a) Yes
   b) Sometimes
   c) No

9) When deciding where to go on holiday, do you ask other people for their opinion?

   a) Often
   b) Sometimes
   c) Never

10) Rather than worrying about a problem do you try to treat it as a challenge?

   a) Yes
   b) Sometimes
   c) No

11) If asked to present the results of a project would you rather:

   a) Give a verbal presentation
   b) Produce a written report

12) A social event has been organised by your company, would you?

   a) Probably attend
   b) Probably not attend

13) Would you rather your colleagues described you as:

   a) Good at your job?
   b) Friendly and well liked?

14) If asked to take part in a group presentation, would you be happy to take centre stage?

   a) Yes
   b) No

15) Would you prefer to work in:

   a) A lively open-plan office?
   b) In an office with the door closed?

16) A colleague at work is late for a meeting, do you:

   a) Hold the meeting in their place?
   b) Cancel the meeting?

17) Would you prefer:

   a) A highly paid but insecure position?
   b) A secure position that is relatively poorly paid?

18) Do you often work late in order to finish projects?

   a) Yes
   b) No

19) When working with computer files do you make a back-up copy?

   a) Every time
   b) Sometimes

20) Which type of projects you've worked on do you consider to have been the most successful?

   a) Group projects
   b) Projects involving only your own work

21) Are you a logical thinker?

   a) Yes
   b) Sometimes
   c) No

22) Do you like to work hard and play hard?

   a) Yes
   b) Sometimes
   c) No

23) Have you ever volunteered to join team projects?

   a) Yes
   b) Sometimes
   c) No

24) Do you like to work on complicated problems?

    a) Yes
    b) Sometimes
    c) No

25) Do you sometimes make impulsive decisions?

    a) Yes
    b) Sometimes
    c) No

26) Do you often socialise with large groups of friends?

    a) Yes
    b) Sometimes
    c) No

27) Do you get nervous before sitting tests?

    a) Yes
    b) Sometimes
    c) No

28) Do you let personal criticism affect your judgement?

    a) Yes
    b) Sometimes
    c) No

29) Practical ideas are more important than abstract theories?

    a) Yes
    b) Sometimes
    c) No

30) Do you enjoy yourself more at work than at home?

    a) Yes
    b) Sometimes
    c) No

Chapter 4

Introduction to Verbal Reasoning Tests

Many jobs involve working with and understanding verbal information, for example, writing letters and memos to colleagues. Above average verbal reasoning abilities become necessary if the job involves writing detailed reports that must be easily understood by work colleagues. Clearly, an understanding of words and how to use them effectively is essential for any graduate or managerial role that includes a focus on written or oral communication. Having a high verbal reasoning ability is vital for working in professions such as journalism and law.

Verbal reasoning tests

Practice examples of four different types of verbal reasoning test (synonyms, analogies, antonyms and word groups) are provided on pages 13 to 20.

Synonyms

The first type consists of a single sentence containing a word in italics. Replace this word with the most viable alternative. Of the five multiple-choice alternatives suggested, select the one that comes closest in meaning to the word in italics.

1) My brother's *complacency* has always irritated his friends, neighbours and colleagues.

   A. nosiness
   B. ostentation
   C. neglect
   D. cockiness
   E. smugness

2) The *ascetic* hermit dwelt in a hut on the mountain top.

   A. austere
   B. religious
   C. penitent
   D. reclusive
   E. indigent

3) The foreign tourists found the locals to be extremely *amiable*.

   A. gracious
   B. friendly
   C. curious
   D. suspicious
   E. polite

4) Parents of pupils complained because they felt that the teacher was too *lenient*.

   A. demanding
   B. strict
   C. tolerant
   D. negligent
   E. informal

5) The King filled his Court with *sycophants* and fops.

   A. courtiers
   B. flatterers
   C. loyalists
   D. advisers
   E. dandies

6) On the flight to New York, he sat next to a very *garrulous* woman.

   A. sullen
   B. attractive
   C. convivial
   D. loud
   E. talkative

7) The tutor praised his students' *perspicacious* comments.

    A. intelligent
    B. insightful
    C. critical
    D. scholarly
    E. technical

8) At the school assembly, the Headmaster sternly declared 'Honesty is a *tenet* of this institution'.

    A. rule
    B. principle
    C. tradition
    D. anathema
    E. virtue

9) The initiates participated in *esoteric* rituals at the midnight ceremony.

    A. ancient
    B. religious
    C. traditional
    D. secret
    E. solemn

10) Investing in the nuclear power industry proved to be the entrepreneur's most *astute* decision.

    A. calculated
    B. risky
    C. controversial
    D. lucrative
    E. shrewd

Analogies

Verbal reasoning tests may also take the form of analogies, where the respondent's vocabulary and knowledge of simple verbal relationships are being tested as part of their overall verbal reasoning ability. Some examples of this type of verbal reasoning test are given below. Interpret the meaning that connects the word shown in large type on the left-hand side (i.e. spider in the first question) with the word shown in small type on the right-hand side (i.e. web). Apply the same verbal reasoning to connect the second word shown in large print on the left-hand side (i.e. rabbit) with one of the multiple-choice answer options.

11) SPIDER ⇨ WEB

RABBIT ⇨ ?

A. FIELD
B. STEW
C. FUR
D. WARREN
E. BARN

12) BOOK ⇨ LIBRARY

PAINTING ⇨ ?

A. GALLERY
B. FRAME
C. EASEL
D. CANVAS
E. SHOP

13) PAPER ⇨ REAM

PAINT ⇨ ?

A. TIN
B. BRUSH
C. TRAY
D. LITRE
E. ACRYLIC

14) BOAT ⇨ WATER

CAR ⇨ ?

A. PETROL
B. ROAD
C. CONVERTIBLE
D. ENGINE
E. TYRES

15) ANIMALS ⇨ HYBRID

METALS ⇨ ?

A. MIXTURE
B. ALLOY
C. COMPOUND
D. BLEND
E. ELEMENT

16) CARPENTER ⇨ LATHE

BLACKSMITH ⇨ ?

A. FORGE
B. METAL
C. IRON
D. ANVIL
E. PLINTH

17) FATHOMLESS ⇨ DEEP

INFINITESIMAL ⇨ ?

A. SHORT
B. LARGE
C. SMALL
D. LONG
E. NARROW

18) LETTER ⇨ ENVELOPE

SWORD ⇨ ?

A. HILT
B. SHEATH
C. WEAPON
D. BLADE
E. DAGGER

19) DECLINE ⇨ ASCENT

CONVICT ⇨ ?

A. LIBERATE
B. ACQUIT
C. INNOCENT
D. PRISONER
E. RELEASE

20) WORDS ⇨ PHRASE

SENTENCES ⇨ ?

A. PARAGRAPH
B. VERSE
C. EPITAPH
D. LETTERS
E. BOOKS

21) INTRODUCTION ⇨ CONCLUSION

PROLOGUE ⇨ ?

A. PREFACE
B. MONOLOGUE
C. EPILOGUE
D. EULOGY
E. FINALE

22) DROUGHT ⇨ RAIN

STALEMATE ⇨ ?

A. DRAW
B. PROGRESS
C. HINDRANCE
D. CESSATION
E. INEQUALITY

23) WORD ⇨ ABBREVIATE

BOOK ⇨ ?

A. EDIT
B. SHORTEN
C. ABRIDGE
D. AMEND
E. COMPRESS

24) PROXY ⇨ VOTE

SCAPEGOAT ⇨ ?

A. VICTIM
B. BLAME
C. TROUBLE
D. CRITIC
E. CENSURE

25) PEANUT ⇨ SHELL

MAIZE ⇨ ?

A. SKIN
B. HUSK
C. RIND
D. PITH
E. POD

26) BICYCLE ⇨ TANDEM

SOLILOQUY ⇨ ?

A. SPEECH
B. MONOLOGUE
C. DIALOGUE
D. DUET
E. SEQUEL

27) WAX ⇨ WANE

AMELIORATE ⇨ ?

A. DIMINISH
B. IMPROVE
C. PROVOKE
D. EXACERBATE
E. IRRITATE

28) CHESS ⇨ BOARD

FOOTBALL ⇨ ?

A. ARENA
B. KIT
C. PITCH
D. GRASS
E. SPORT

29) BIBLIOPHILE ⇨ BOOKS

PHILATELIST ⇨ ?

A. COINS
B. WINE
C. STAMPS
D. DOLLS
E. ART

30) FLAX ⇨ LINEN

WHEAT ⇨ ?

A. GRAIN
B. CEREAL
C. BREAD
D. CORN
E. SHEAF

Antonyms

Verbal reasoning tests may also take the form of antonyms. An antonym is a word which means the exact opposite of another word. Some examples of this type of verbal reasoning test are given below. Select the multiple-choice option that is the opposite in meaning to the word shown in bold print.

31) **mean**	A	B	C	D	E
	generous	average	miser	median	good

	A	B	C	D	E
32) **sincere**	faithful	hypocritical	genuine	suspicious	unkind
33) **evergreen**	myrtle	flower	deciduous	fern	yellow
34) **irresponsible**	mischievous	independent	diplomatic	dependable	manager
35) **nationalisation**	democracy	oligopoly	coalition	trains	privatisation
36) **inauspicious**	lucky	auspices	bachelor	mutinous	inarticulate
37) **pessimism**	pesticide	optimism	prototype	positive	socialism
38) **innocuous**	vaccinate	amicable	harmful	ostensible	effusive
39) **benevolent**	kind	empirical	demagogue	uncharitable	eminent
40) **altruistic**	bird	helpful	unhelpful	altitude	selfish

Word Groups

Verbal reasoning tests may also take the form of selecting the odd word out from a group of words. Some examples of this type of verbal reasoning test are given below. Identify the common connection between four of the five words and then choose the multiple-choice option corresponding to the odd word out.

	A	B	C	D	E
41)	magenta	cyan	cerise	turpentine	turquoise

	A	B	C	D	E
42)	sole	haddock	salmon	trout	frog
43)	damp	wet	water	moist	saturated
44)	staff	personnel	employees	workforce	managers
45)	jester	comedian	comedy	clown	comedienne
46)	photocopy	computer	letter	memo	email
47)	hexagon	polygon	pentagon	octagon	square
48)	squid	cockle	mussel	crab	winkle
49)	trophy	medal	prize	gift	reward
50)	cask	beer	bottle	can	barrel

Introduction to comprehension assessments (verbal reasoning in context)

Many graduate and managerial job roles require employees to extract quickly relevant information from written documents and to make a judgement based on this information. Comprehension assessments (verbal reasoning tests in context) measure the ability to read and interpret a detailed block of text under timed conditions. Graduate and managerial-level questions tend to consist of single sections of text, each of which is followed by a series of questions relating to that particular section. Each question requires relevant pieces of information to be extracted from the passage and a specific judgement to be made on the basis of this information. This test format is somewhat similar to a traditional reading comprehension test, since it checks the reader's understanding of a written passage by asking questions on the themes contained within a particular passage.

Answering the questions correctly requires an objective perspective to be taken, without any interference from the candidate's own beliefs about the subject matter. Similarly only the information contained within the passage should be used to answer each question, without recourse to any prior general knowledge about the subject matter concerned.

Comprehension questions

The comprehension questions below consist of a long passage of text, followed by two or three statements about the information contained within the passage. Identify which of these statements are 'correct' and which statements are 'incorrect'. Only use the information given in the passages. Assume that the information in the passages is correct even if you know otherwise.

The term Pre-Raphaelite is somewhat confusing, as it refers to a British Victorian art movement rather than a 15th-century Italian school of painting. In 1848, a group of seven young artists, including Dante Gabriel Rossetti, William Holman Hunt and John Everett Millais, founded an aesthetic movement, dubbing themselves the Pre-Raphaelite Brotherhood. Espousing the style of painters before the time of Raphael, they rejected the technique of chiaroscuro and what they saw to be the artificiality of the Renaissance Great Masters. Although the members of the Pre-Raphaelite Brotherhood had highly individualistic styles, there were certain tenets shared by the group. Their paintings often featured religious, mythical or symbolic subjects. Paying meticulous attention to detail and striving for truth in art, the Pre-Raphaelites painted directly from nature and used ordinary people as their models. Admiring the bright, flat colours of the Italian painters of the Quattrocento, Pre-Raphaelites painted over a white, wet ground to achieve brilliant colours. Their early works were disliked by both the public and the Academy. Charles Dickens was particularly vociferous in his contempt for the Pre-Raphaelites' work. However, John Ruskin, the eminent Victorian art critic, championed the Pre-Raphaelite cause and paved their entry into the art establishment. While the founding members of the Pre-Raphaelite Brotherhood splintered into various directions, their legacy influenced a younger generation of English painters, and their works are still enormously popular today.

QUESTIONS:

51) John Ruskin was a more important art critic than Charles Dickens.

52) The Pre-Raphaelites were concerned with realism and honesty, wanting to depict ordinary people.

53) The Pre-Raphaelites' criticisms of the Italian Great Masters were of a stylistic nature, rather than objections about the paintings thematic content.

OPTIONS:
A. Correct
B. Incorrect

Cinema recently celebrated its 100th anniversary. A multi-million dollar business, cinema is the United States' second largest industry, second only to aeronautics. However, today's blockbuster Hollywood films, with their dazzling computer-generated special effects, would not have been possible without the pioneering work of Edward Muybridge in the late 19th century. An English photographer, Muybridge photographed sequences of animals and humans running and walking. He invented a device called a succession, creating an illusion of movement. Films today are shot on 35mm film and shown through a projector, which operates in a similar manner to Muybridge's invention. A typical feature-length film uses 2.5km (1.5 miles) of film, which runs through the projector at a rate of 8 frames per second. Although Muybridge's experiments did not feature sound, plot, colour or movie stars, his vision paved the way for an entire industry.

QUESTIONS:

54) Feature films today can use several kilometres of film.

55) Edward Muybridge has a place in cinema history as a pioneer.

56) The zoogyroscope was the precursor to the modern movie camera.

OPTIONS:
A. Correct
B. Incorrect

Graphology, the analysis of handwriting, has been studied since ancient Greek times, but it was not until the 19th century that the first modern theoretical works on the subject were published. A person's handwriting is a form of self-expression and can be used to discern various psychological traits. Although many people are suspicious of graphology's reliability, it has several practical applications and is widely used. In police investigations, graphology is often used to help compile a suspect's psychological profile. Many employers request handwritten covering letters to study applicants' characters, though the practice is not popular with candidates. The slant of a person's letters can indicate their emotional stability. Left-slanting penmanship can mean defensiveness or repression of emotions, while right-slanting writing suggests friendliness and discipline. The slope of the writing is also revealing. Upward sloping writing shows optimism, whereas descending lines demonstrate pessimism, or even ill health. The document as a whole must also be considered, examining factors such as margins, line spacing and pressure. A wide left margin is a sign of extroversion, while introverts tend to leave a narrow left margin. A person's signature is very telling, expressing how they wish to be perceived by others. A signature that differs from the rest of a person's writing suggests dishonesty. The size of a signature demonstrates a person's self-importance or lack of self-worth. Graphology does have its limitations. It cannot be used to tell a person's age, gender or profession. However, used correctly, graphology can be a powerful analytical tool, providing valuable insight into certain character traits.

QUESTIONS:

57) While graphology is an inadequate means of assessing a person's socio-economic status, experts can use it to compile a complete psychological profile.

58) There is rarely one single interpretation for any given handwriting characteristic.

59) Graphology was not studied prior to 1800.

OPTIONS:
A. Correct
B. Incorrect

The questionnaire contained a number of statements and questions concerned with pupils' perceptions of their parents' attitude to school and education. The questionnaire results were correlated with pupil performance. The results showed that there is a strong relationship between children's perceptions of their parental attitudes to school and the performance of their children in school. It was surmised that if parents have a negative attitude to education then their children are reluctant to learn at school. It may be the case that these children are also lacking intellectual stimulation in their home environments.

QUESTIONS:

60) The parents filled in the questionnaire.

61) The relationship between pupils' school performance and their perceptions of their parents' attitude to school was explored.

OPTIONS:
A. Correct
B. Incorrect

Editors are not just glorified spell-checkers. They have to ensure that text is grammatically correct. They have to check that typesetters and artists have produced material that is in line with the specification they were given. An editor must clarify that all artwork and tables are in the correct place. It is also vital that they check that every aspect of a product adheres to company standards. They liaise with many internal and external contacts including authors, product managers and production controllers.

QUESTIONS:

62) Editors can ignore company standards when they consider it appropriate.

63) An editor must check that artwork is in the correct position.

OPTIONS:
A. Correct
B. Incorrect

New theories about the origins of the pyramids of Egypt point to ancient and unknown civilisations being the original builders. New Age investigators talk in the same breath of the great pyramid of Cheops and the lost city of Atlantis. They argue that the precision and alignment of these undoubtedly awe-inspiring structures are clear evidence that the original architects were holders of arcane knowledge far beyond our own. However, mainstream Egyptologists look on the current wave of para-archaeology with disdain. As an example they point to the weathering of the Sphinx. New Agers point to the fact that the body of the Sphinx has been weathered by water which indicates it existed through a long temperate period in Egypt's history. The refutation of this argument is that millennia underneath the desert sands would have a similar weathering effect.

QUESTIONS:

64) The origin of the pyramids of Egypt is still controversial.

65) The millennia underneath the desert sands have been weathered.

OPTIONS:
A. Correct
B. Incorrect

Chapter 5

Introduction to Numerical Reasoning Tests

Numeracy skills and the ability to understand information presented in various numerical formats are essential for any graduate and managerial role with a numerical component. These skills can be assessed by numerical reasoning tests which measure the ability to reason with numbers and to solve numerical problems. The simplest level of numerical reasoning tests is number series where the test taker must work out the relationship between a sequence of numbers. More advanced numerical reasoning tests may present the information in context with a short introduction about the numerical scenario – as would occur when using numerical skills in the workplace.

Numerical reasoning tests

This section starts with some practice examples of number series. Identify the number that fits the space in a sequence of numbers. Since the practice questions that follow are aimed at a graduate and managerial level, it is worth remembering that they may involve more than just the four basic mathematical operations of addition, subtraction, division and multiplication.

1) 1664   824   404   194   ?

	A	B	C	D	E
	89	365	44	45	46

2) 3   9   36   ?   1080

	A	B	C	D	E
	130	131	180	181	360

3) 7   18   47   ?   322

	A	B	C	D	E
	100	123	127	137	143

4)   20   33   59   111   ?

	A	B	C	D	E
	149	153	169	176	215

5)   12   34   78   ?   342

	A	B	C	D	E
	166	168	183	184	187

6)   9   16   45   176   ?

	A	B	C	D	E
	868	870	873	875	880

7)   −88   −48   −8   ?

	A	B	C	D	E
	32	−18	−8	18	−56

8)   9   19   34   59   ?

	A	B	C	D	E
	99	89	84	79	74

9)   6   30   120   360   ?

	A	B	C	D	E
	720	840	980	1080	1440

10)   6   9   13.5   20.25   ?

	A	B	C	D	E
	30	30.25	30.375	30.5	30.75

11)   3   9   ?   486   5832

	A	B	C	D	E
	18	27	54	72	81

12)   −¾   0   ½   1¼   ?

	A	B	C	D	E
	1	1½	1¾	2	2¼

13) 7   12   19   ?   39   52

	A	B	C	D	E
	21	25	26	28	29

14) 96   ?   85   70   50   25

	A	B	C	D	E
	87	89	91	93	95

15) 11   7   22   21   ?   35   44

	A	B	C	D	E
	23	25	26	31	33

16) 343   216   125   ?   27

	A	B	C	D	E
	64	56	49	36	33

17) −3   −1   3   9   ?   27

	A	B	C	D	E
	13	14	15	17	23

18) 82   17   73   34   ?   68   55

	A	B	C	D	E
	46	51	56	60	64

19) 208   195   169   ?   78   13

	A	B	C	D	E
	143	130	125	118	104

20) 4/9   2/3   1   ?   9/4   27/8

	A	B	C	D	E
	5/4	3/2	7/4	2	17/8

21) 42   22   ?   7   4.5   3.25

	A	B	C	D	E
	9	10	12	15	18

22)   −5   −19   −61   −187   ?

	A	B	C	D	E
	−246	−248	−561	−565	−568

23)   5   8   17   44   ?

	A	B	C	D	E
	52	61	62	98	125

24)   5   13   29   61   ?

	A	B	C	D	E
	74	87	90	122	125

25)   1   12   45   ?   441

	A	B	C	D	E
	134	135	137	144	147

26)   75   300   150   100   300   ?

	A	B	C	D	E
	200	150	100	75	33.3

27)   7   6   42   42   252   ?

	A	B	C	D	E
	252	262	294	326	336

28)   384   48   ?   2   1

	A	B	C	D	E
	4	6	8	10	12

29)   1   3   4   7   ?

	A	B	C	D	E
	9	10	11	12	13

30)   249   209   179   159   ?

	A	B	C	D	E
	149	153	169	176	199

Introduction to numerical reasoning tests (in context)

Within the workplace, numerical information can be encountered in a variety of formats. Specific information may need to be extracted and interpreted from graphs, tables or pie charts in order to make recommendations or to write a comprehensive report. It is therefore important to assess the numerical reasoning ability of graduates and managers in a variety of different contexts.

The following practice questions reflect the different demands made by sets of numerical information. When attempting the questions, remember to round up any decimal points and any pence where necessary.

Numerical reasoning questions (in context)

The simple and compound interest added on to £100.00 after five years are shown in the table below.

YEARLY RATE	SIMPLE	COMPOUND
7%	£35.00	£40.26
8%	£40.00	£46.93
9%	£45.00	£53.86
10%	£50.00	£61.05

31) What would the total compound interest be on £200.00 at a rate of 8% over five years?

A	B	C	D	E
£107.72	£93.86	£87.19	£80.52	£88.00

32) How much extra is earned in compound interest, compared to simple interest, on £300.00 at 9% over five years?

A	B	C	D	E
£18.86	£13.29	£26.58	£27.28	£53.86

33) What is the difference between the compound rate of interest earned on £200.00 at 7% to 9% over five years?

A	B	C	D	E
£26.40	£26.80	£27.60	£27.20	£27.00

The table below shows the population of six countries, together with the population density for each country.

COUNTRY	POPULATION (millions)	POPULATION DENSITY (people per km²)
Australia	17.8	2
Canada	27.8	3
Japan	125.0	331
Sweden	8.7	21
UK	57.8	239
US	257.8	28

34) What is the total area of Japan in square kilometres (10,000s)?

A	B	C	D	E
264.0	37.8	206.0	26.4	378.0

35) What is the difference between the populations of Canada and the US combined, and Japan and Australia combined?

A	B	C	D	E
115.0	132.8	142.8	257.8	267.8

36) If the Japanese population increased by 4 per cent annually over the next two years, what would its population be in two years' time?

A	B	C	D	E
135.20	135.25	135.40	135.35	135.30

The table below shows the approximate flight distances of major airports from London.

COUNTRY	DISTANCE (km)
ATHENS	2400
CAIRO	3500
CHICAGO	6300
MADRID	1200
MEXICO CITY	9000
NEW YORK	5500
RIO DE JANEIRO	9200
SYDNEY	17000

37) If it takes approximately 10 hours to fly to Chicago from London, then how many hours would it take to fly to Sydney? (Assume that the same plane travels at the same average speed to each destination.)

A	B	C	D	E
25	26	27	28	29

38) A flight from London to Rio de Janeiro is re-routed to Mexico City. In kilometres what is the difference in the flight distance now flown by the plane?

A	B	C	D	E
200 less	100 less	100 more	200 more	500 more

39) Two planes leave London half an hour apart. The first plane to leave arrives in Mexico City 15 hours later at 04.00. If both planes fly at the same speed, when does the second plane arrive in Rio de Janeiro?

A	B	C	D	E
04.00	04.15	04.20	04.25	04.50

In a wrapping paper factory the size of paper is given in terms of X, Y and Z.
X = 3Y, and 2Y = 9Z.

40) If a sheet of paper is 2X long, then how long is it in terms of Z?

A	B	C	D	E
27Z	18Z	9Z	12Z	6Z

41) If it costs £6.48 to produce a roll of paper 54Z long, how much does it cost to produce a roll of paper 6X long?

A	B	C	D	E
£12.96	£3.24	£9.72	£1.08	£4.32

42) If Y = 10cm, then what is the area of a piece of paper, in metres squared, that is 2Y long and 2X wide?

A	B	C	D	E
12.00	0.12	18.00	1.20	1.80

Some of the plans for a new shopping mall are shown below.

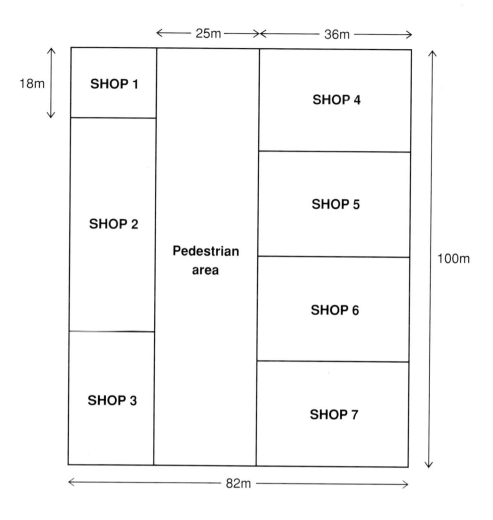

43) What is the total shop-floor space of all seven shops combined?

A	B	C	D	E
3600m²	5700m²	2500m²	8200m²	4500m²

44) Shops 4, 5, 6 and 7 are all the same area, what is the area of shop 6?

A	B	C	D	E
870m²	880m²	360m²	950m²	900m²

45) Shop 2 is three times as large as shop 1. What is the area of shop 3?

A	B	C	D	E
588m²	600m²	554m²	615m²	620m²

The pie chart shows the proportion of income spent by a taxi-driver per month. The taxi-driver earns £24,000 a year net of tax.

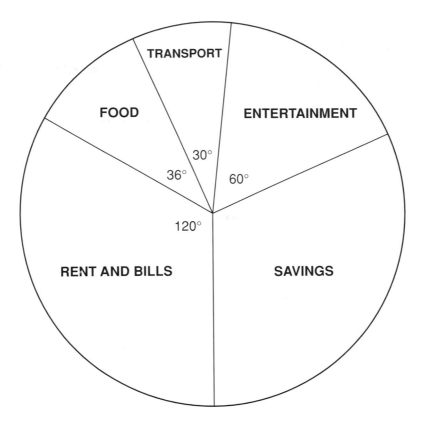

46) How much is spent on food per month?

A	B	C	D	E
£275	£250	£200	£180	£300

47) How much more per month is spent on entertainment than transport?

A	B	C	D	E
£166.67	£190.67	£196.33	£333.33	£266.67

48) How much does the taxi-driver save per month?

A	B	C	D	E
£900	£633	£312	£450	£518

The price of Newwill Building Society shares is shown for the five trading days Monday to Friday.

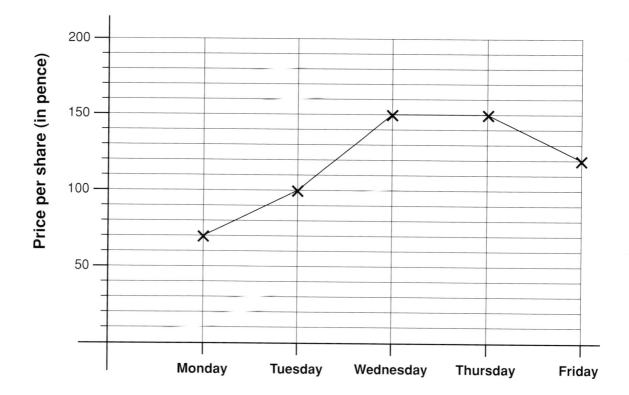

49) A trader bought 100 Newwill shares on Wednesday and sold all these shares on Friday. How much had the value of the investment changed?

A	B	C	D	E
Lost £250	Lost £30	Gained £20	Gained £25	Lost £20

50) A businessman bought 200 shares on Tuesday and sold 100 the next day. How much cash profit was made on Wednesday?

A	B	C	D	E
£5.00	£5.50	£100	£50	£10

51) If I had bought 50 Newwill shares on Monday and 50 on Tuesday, how much would the total shareholding be worth on the Friday?

A	B	C	D	E
£75	£110	£120	£250	£225

Company X conducted a survey to find the method(s) of transport used by employees to get to work.

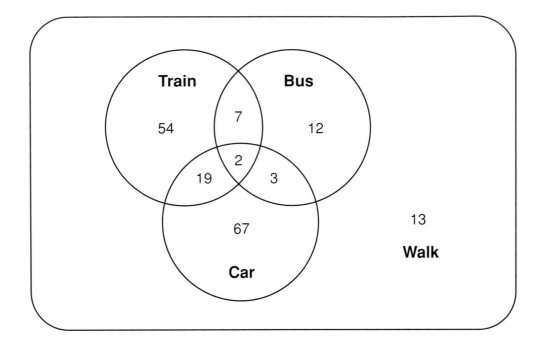

52) What is the total number of people who travel by car for ONLY part of their journey?

A	B	C	D	E
24	92	67	82	91

53) How many people use both a bus and a train (but not a car)?

A	B	C	D	E
75	2	9	7	66

54) What is the total number of people in the company (excluding those living within walking distance)?

A	B	C	D	E
177	133	164	146	178

Below are pie charts showing the proportion of pigs, sheep and cows in three villages.

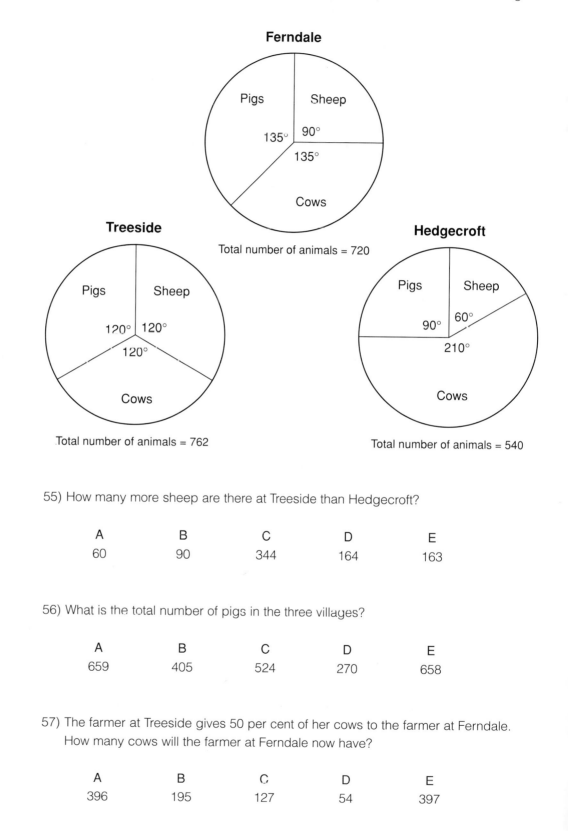

Ferndale

Pigs 135°

Sheep 90°

135°

Cows

Total number of animals = 720

Treeside

Pigs 120°

Sheep 120°

120°

Cows

Total number of animals = 762

Hedgecroft

Pigs 90°

Sheep 60°

210°

Cows

Total number of animals = 540

55) How many more sheep are there at Treeside than Hedgecroft?

A	B	C	D	E
60	90	344	164	163

56) What is the total number of pigs in the three villages?

A	B	C	D	E
659	405	524	270	658

57) The farmer at Treeside gives 50 per cent of her cows to the farmer at Ferndale. How many cows will the farmer at Ferndale now have?

A	B	C	D	E
396	195	127	54	397

The graph below shows the total land area (in 100,000s of square kilometres) for each of the seven countries in Central America.

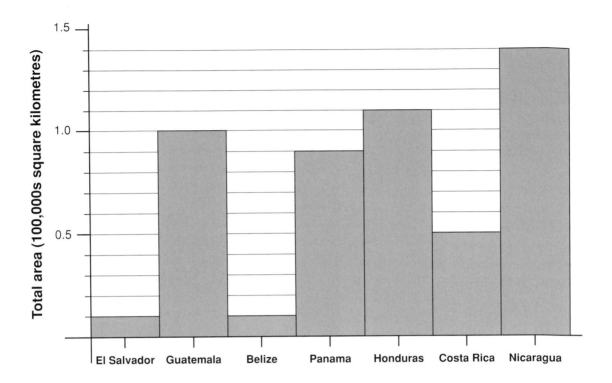

58) What is the total area of the seven Central American countries (in 100,000s of square kilometres)?

A	B	C	D	E
4.0	4.6	4.9	5.1	5.3

59) What is the difference (in 100,000s square kilometres) between the two largest and the two smallest countries?

A	B	C	D	E
1.8	1.9	2.0	2.1	2.3

60) There are 2.59 square kilometres in one square mile. How many times larger is Nicaragua than Costa Rica?

A	B	C	D	E
3.1	2.8	3.3	2.3	3.5

Chapter 6

Introduction to Clerical Tests

When applying for a position requiring skills such as report writing and assimilating information quickly a graduate or manager may be asked to sit some form of clerical test. The ability to check and classify information accurately helps keep communication clear and effective within an office environment. Clerical work in general involves numerous different skills, in particular being able to process detailed information accurately. A written test that closely follows the clerical demands of a particular job may be better described as a 'job sample' rather than a generic clerical test.

One useful clerical skill is knowing how to spell words correctly and the ability to recognise misspelt words – even though spell-checks are now freely available! Spelling test questions may take the form of the examples shown below, where each section contains an unspecified number of misspelt words to be identified. Underline all the words in each paragraph which appear misspelt and write the correct spelling above each one.

Clerical questions

1) The patient entered the clinic feeling pesimistic and subdued. The therapist sytemetically attempted to alliviate her patient's excrutiating pain. The patient was very grateful for her therapist's time and patence.

2) The professer conducted her innovative research in a sound-proof laboratory. The details of the research are highly confedential. The launch of her amazing discovery is scheduled for the forteenth of Febuary.

3) It is proposed that the traffic-calming scheme will be completed this autunm. Some residants of the neghbouring village are petitioning against the scheme. They are worried that it may increase the number of vechiles coming through their streets.

4) The athletics championships is an event which unites the whole word into competition. Partcipants can be multi-disciplined in a variety of major events, spaning everything from discus-throwing to relay-running.

5) This has been the most dreadful storm this millenium. The torrantial rain is causing chaos. Thousands of devestated families have had to evacuate their homes.

6) The farocious leopard scoured its home terrain looking for its pray. A petrified antelope was paralysed with fear as the leoperd steathily launched its attacking ritual.

7) Your cycling proficiancy test will take place next month. It is advisible to recap on your Highway Code in the time leading up to your test. Remember, it is imperative to put safety first.

8) The stationary cupboard door must always be kept shut and locked. This is a fire percaution. The key is available from reception. Always return the key straigth away as others may need it.

9) The statistical tables show the values of the cummulative distribution functions. They also contain probability dencity functions of certain common distributions for different values of their parametres.

10) Volunteer conservationalists worked through the night in a desparate attempt to rectify the damage from the storm. They specialies in rebuilding fences and moving debrie from pathways.

11) He is committed wholehertedly to the values and beliefs of the new movement. Already his dedication to the promotion of our policies has made a significant impact in our local area. Therefore please vote for him as our new president in the comittee elections next month.

12) The punghent dark red, poisenous liquid is used in pesticedes. Some recent scientific research has shown that if it comes into contact with human skin it causes an itchey rash.

13) The tenacious production manager was not respected by the majority of her disilusioned staff. The personnel department brought this matter to her attention in her annual preformance appraisal.

14) The impressive new gymnaisium contains the most up-to-date equipement. Individuals wishing to make use of this new facility are encouraged to have an induction. Fitness tests are also recomended.

15) It was her fortieth birthday. She had purchased an exquisite new dress and some jewelery for the occason. Her happiness was truly visable as she danced gayly to the rhythmn of the music.

16) A new chimny-pot was required to create a greater draught. In addition, the mantlepiece needed replacing. Therefore they decided it was more financialy viable to invest in an electric fire.

17) Although he always excelled in his Maths class, in English he was prone to mispell a large proportion of words. His vocabulary was also limited and his writing ilegible. It is recommended that he attends remedial English classes.

18) Any perishible items obtained from the delicatesen should be refrigerated immediately. Raw and cooked meat should always be stored separetely. All products should be consumed by the date stated.

19) The endurence test required competitors to tolerate extreme physical challenge. One potental problem being that the weather forcast had predicted rain and strong winds.

20) The immaculate appartment was bursting with antiques, and various other treasures he had acumulated from his world-wide travels. He claimed the most precious items were those with sentimental value.

Chapter 7

Introduction to Non-Verbal Reasoning Tests

Within today's constantly changing workplace, new concepts and ideas need to be acquired readily and then easily assimilated with one's existing knowledge. Flexibility of thinking is fundamental for understanding and assimilating new information and experiencing situations that have not been encountered before. Such skills are used whenever people learn, and allow new material to be related to what is already known. While graduates and managers must be able to implement business-focused solutions, the stages of thinking that lead up to reaching that solution may be equally important. Non-verbal reasoning test scores provide an indication of learning potential. Non-verbal reasoning assessments which ask the individual to find patterns in a series of shapes give an indication of both their ability to reason logically and also their ability to understand new 'ideas'. In broader terms, non-verbal reasoning assessments measure a general ability for critical thinking.

Having a minimal amount of verbal content, non-verbal reasoning tests provide a test which is relatively independent of language skills. Usually comprising only of shapes, such as squares, triangles and circles, without any verbal or numerical content, non-verbal reasoning tests may also be easily confused with abstract reasoning tests.

In the practice questions that follow, identify the logical patterns within the sequence of squares in each grid, then decide which of the multiple-choice options is the most appropriate for the empty square in the grid.

Non-verbal reasoning questions

1)

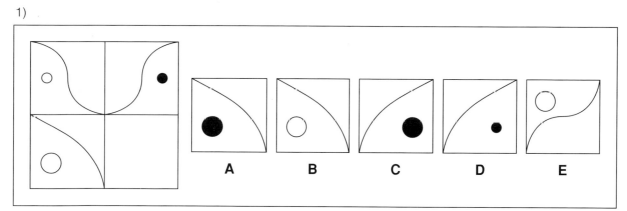

2)

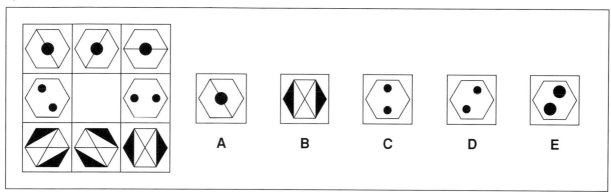

3)

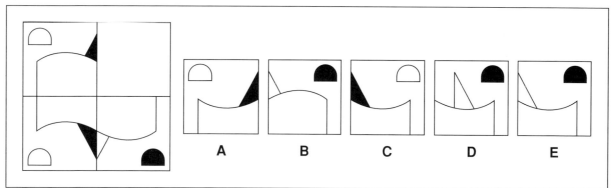

4)

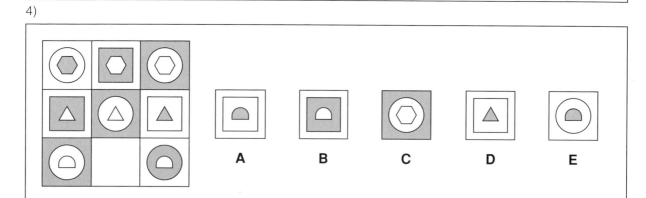

5)

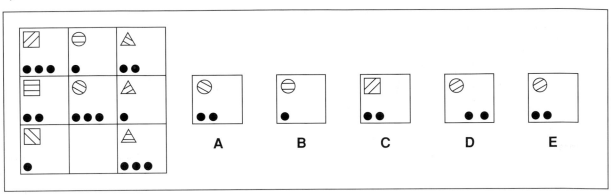

6)

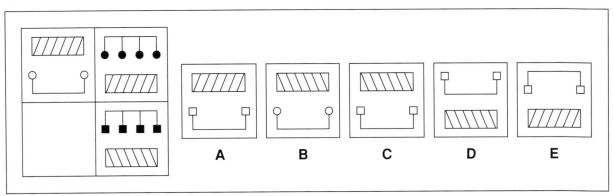

7)

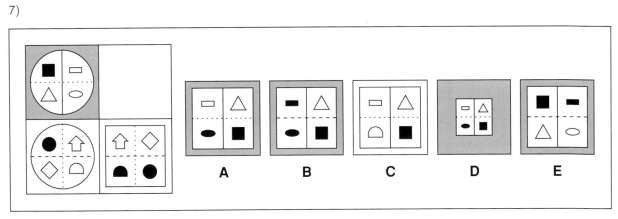

8)

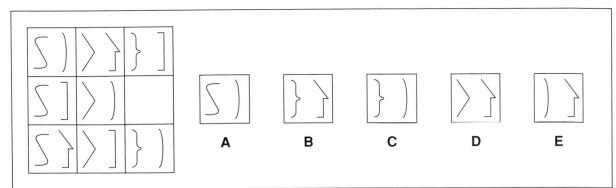

9)

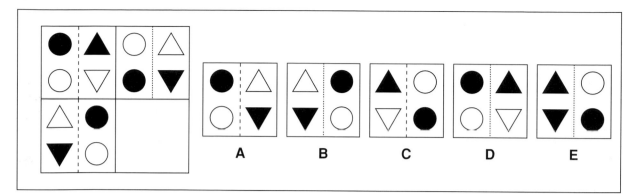

10)

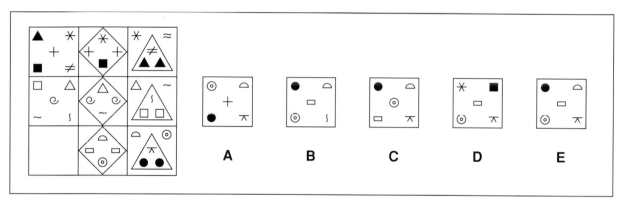

11)

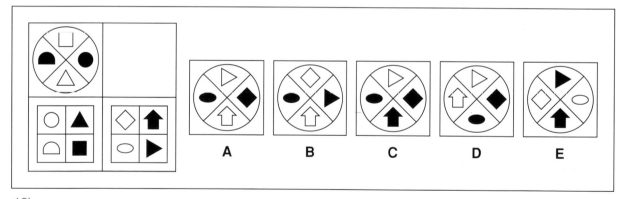

12)

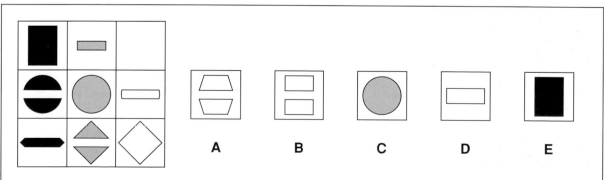

13)

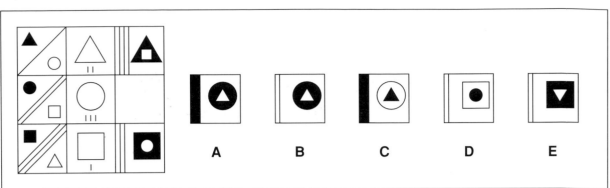

14)

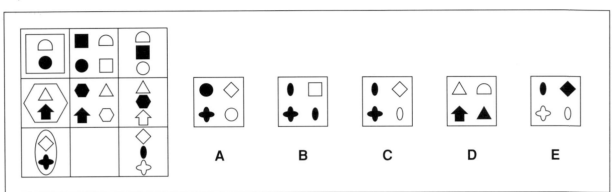

15)

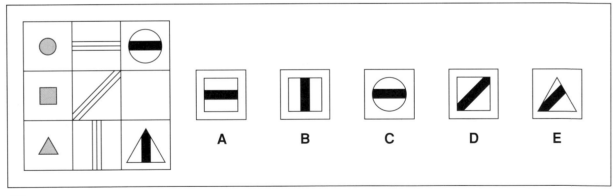

16)

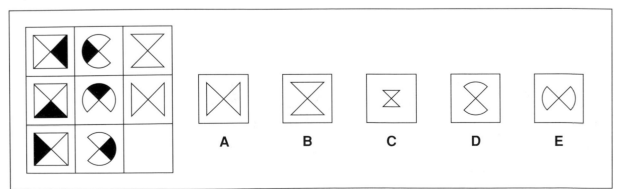

17)

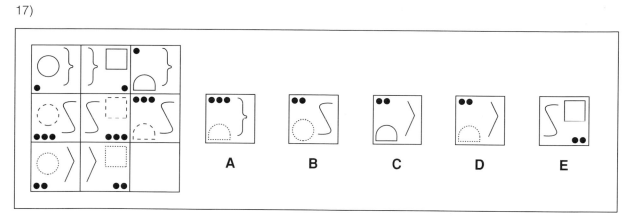

18)

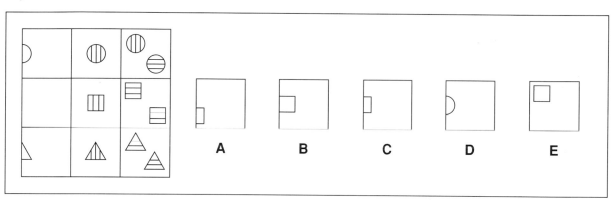

19)

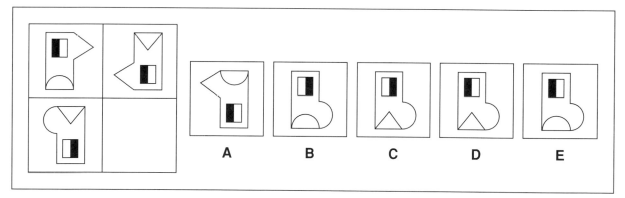

20)

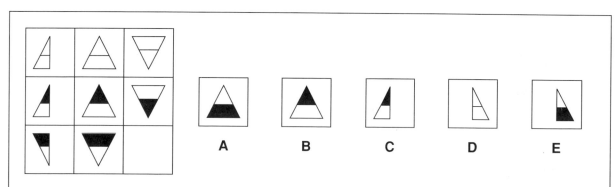

Chapter 8

Introduction to Mechanical Reasoning Tests

Mechanical reasoning tests focus on the understanding of basic mechanical principles. They assess an individual's ability to visualise how a whole mechanical system operates and to understand the relationship between each individual moving part in the system. Questions tend to be based on the effect on the overall system of changes in individual parts. In addition to mechanical knowledge, a more general reasoning ability is important for success at such tests. Understanding the ways in which mechanical systems operate is a vital requirement for all engineering and mechanical disciplines.

If these questions prove problematic, it may be advisable to refer back to appropriate text books before attempting them in a job selection context. The practice questions shown below are typical of the mechanical reasoning questions that a graduate or manager is likely to encounter.

Mechanical reasoning questions

1) A crowbar is used to lift a load (below). Which crowbar makes lifting the load easiest?

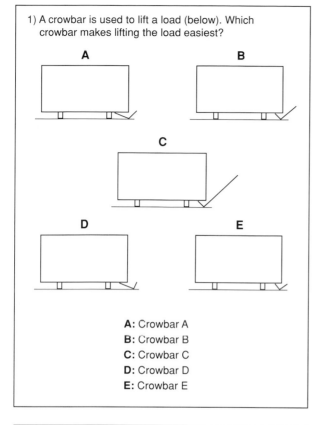

A: Crowbar A
B: Crowbar B
C: Crowbar C
D: Crowbar D
E: Crowbar E

2) Which person exerts the least pressure on the platform?

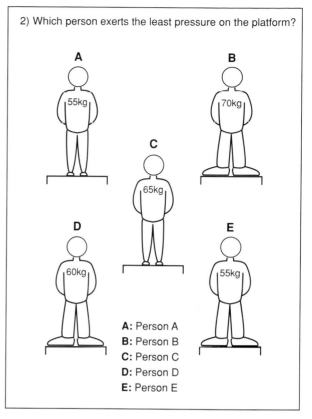

A: Person A
B: Person B
C: Person C
D: Person D
E: Person E

3) If the ball at point P moves up and down and makes waves in the water tank, at which point would the waves travel fastest?

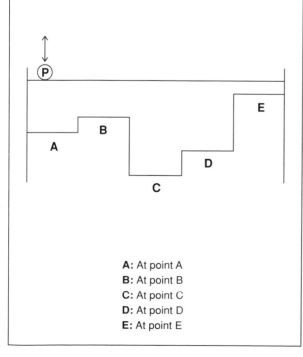

A: At point A
B: At point B
C: At point C
D: At point D
E: At point E

4) For the plank to be balanced, which of the following statements is true?

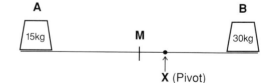

A: X would have to be half way along the plank, at M
B: X would have to be half way between M and B
C: X would have to be half way between M and A
D: X would have to be two-thirds of the way along the plank from A
E: X would have to be two-thirds of the way along the plank from B

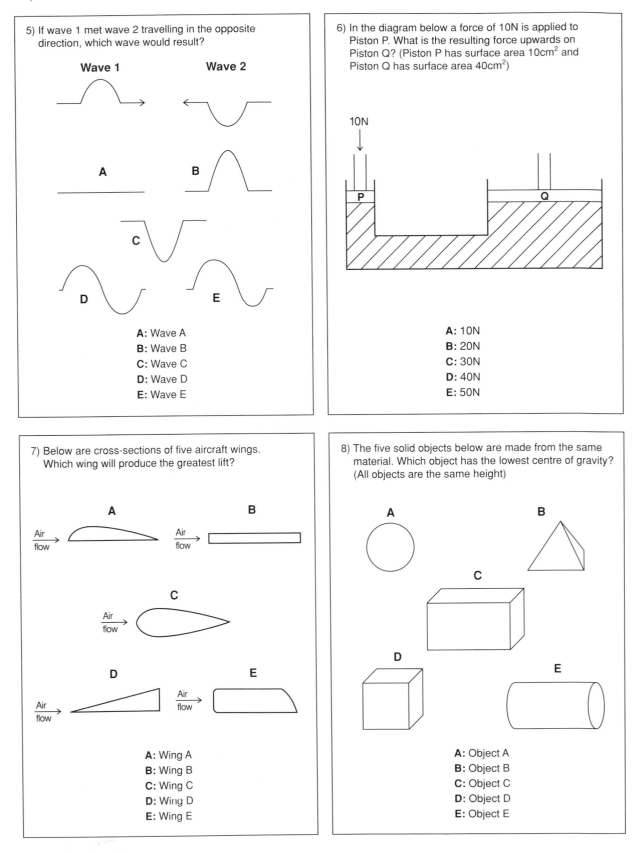

5) If wave 1 met wave 2 travelling in the opposite direction, which wave would result?

Wave 1   **Wave 2**

A

B

C

D   E

A: Wave A
B: Wave B
C: Wave C
D: Wave D
E: Wave E

6) In the diagram below a force of 10N is applied to Piston P. What is the resulting force upwards on Piston Q? (Piston P has surface area 10cm^2 and Piston Q has surface area 40cm^2)

10N

P   Q

A: 10N
B: 20N
C: 30N
D: 40N
E: 50N

7) Below are cross-sections of five aircraft wings. Which wing will produce the greatest lift?

A   B
Air flow   Air flow

C
Air flow

D   E
Air flow   Air flow

A: Wing A
B: Wing B
C: Wing C
D: Wing D
E: Wing E

8) The five solid objects below are made from the same material. Which object has the lowest centre of gravity? (All objects are the same height)

A   B

C

D   E

A: Object A
B: Object B
C: Object C
D: Object D
E: Object E

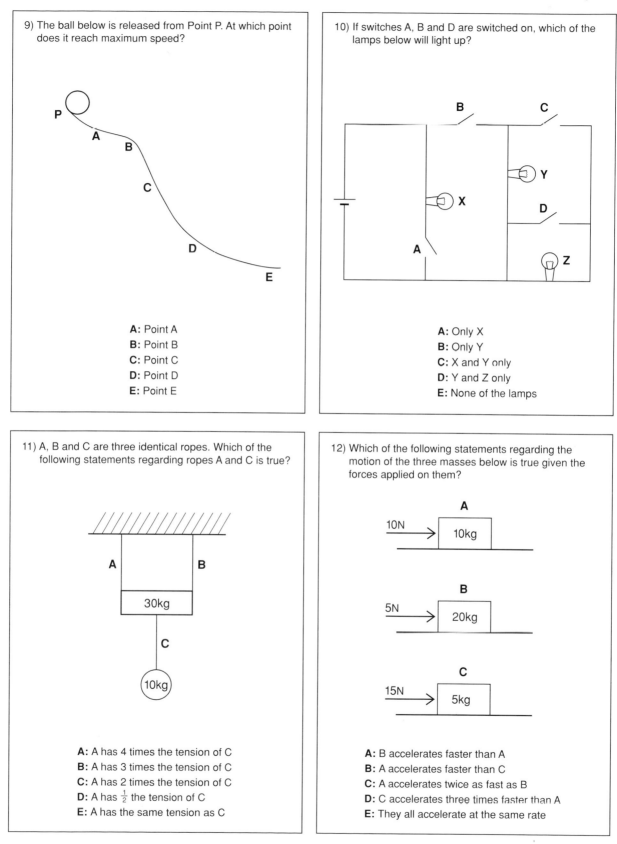

9) The ball below is released from Point P. At which point does it reach maximum speed?

P
A
B
C
D
E

A: Point A
B: Point B
C: Point C
D: Point D
E: Point E

10) If switches A, B and D are switched on, which of the lamps below will light up?

B   C
Y
X
A   D
Z

A: Only X
B: Only Y
C: X and Y only
D: Y and Z only
E: None of the lamps

11) A, B and C are three identical ropes. Which of the following statements regarding ropes A and C is true?

A   B
30kg
C
10kg

A: A has 4 times the tension of C
B: A has 3 times the tension of C
C: A has 2 times the tension of C
D: A has $\frac{1}{2}$ the tension of C
E: A has the same tension as C

12) Which of the following statements regarding the motion of the three masses below is true given the forces applied on them?

A
10N → 10kg

B
5N → 20kg

C
15N → 5kg

A: B accelerates faster than A
B: A accelerates faster than C
C: A accelerates twice as fast as B
D: C accelerates three times faster than A
E: They all accelerate at the same rate

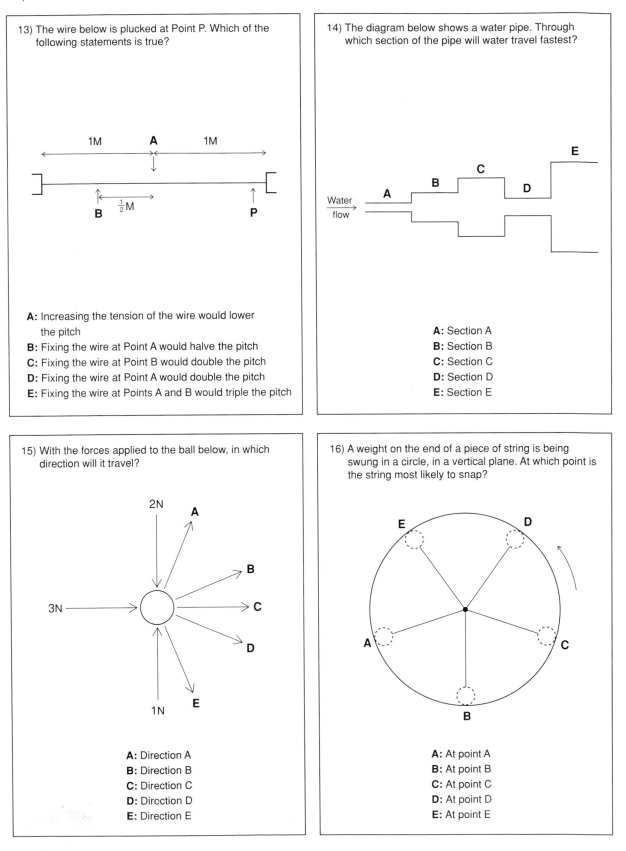

13) The wire below is plucked at Point P. Which of the following statements is true?

1M   **A**   1M

B $\frac{1}{2}$M   **P**

A: Increasing the tension of the wire would lower the pitch
B: Fixing the wire at Point A would halve the pitch
C: Fixing the wire at Point B would double the pitch
D: Fixing the wire at Point A would double the pitch
E: Fixing the wire at Points A and B would triple the pitch

14) The diagram below shows a water pipe. Through which section of the pipe will water travel fastest?

E

C

B   **D**

A

Water flow

A: Section A
B: Section B
C: Section C
D: Section D
E: Section E

15) With the forces applied to the ball below, in which direction will it travel?

2N
A
B
3N   **C**
D
1N   **E**

A: Direction A
B: Direction B
C: Direction C
D: Direction D
E: Direction E

16) A weight on the end of a piece of string is being swung in a circle, in a vertical plane. At which point is the string most likely to snap?

E   **D**

A   **C**

B

A: At point A
B: At point B
C: At point C
D: At point D
E: At point E

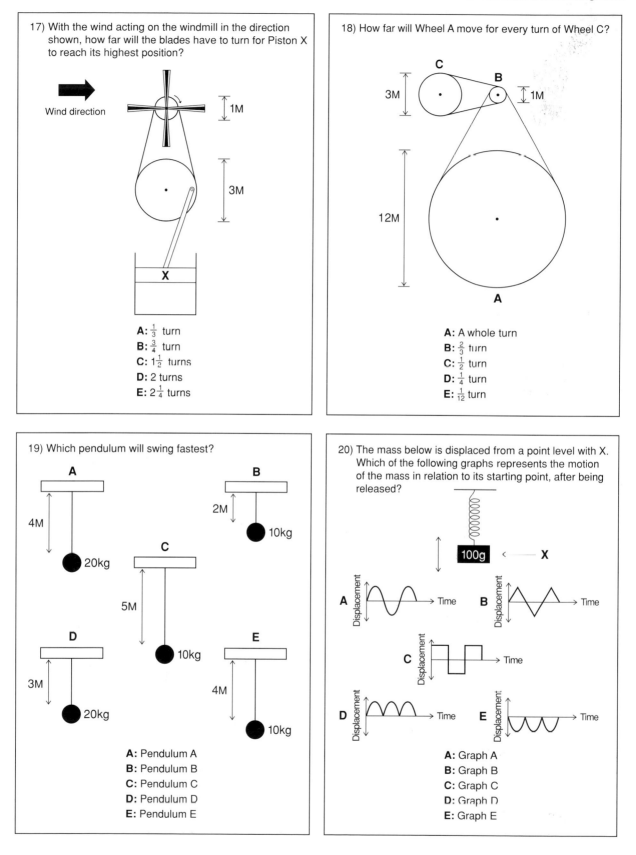

17) With the wind acting on the windmill in the direction shown, how far will the blades have to turn for Piston X to reach its highest position?

Wind direction

1M

3M

X

A: $\frac{1}{3}$ turn
B: $\frac{3}{4}$ turn
C: $1\frac{1}{2}$ turns
D: 2 turns
E: $2\frac{1}{4}$ turns

18) How far will Wheel A move for every turn of Wheel C?

C

B

3M

1M

12M

A

A: A whole turn
B: $\frac{2}{3}$ turn
C: $\frac{1}{2}$ turn
D: $\frac{1}{4}$ turn
E: $\frac{1}{12}$ turn

19) Which pendulum will swing fastest?

A

4M

20kg

B

2M

10kg

C

5M

10kg

D

3M

20kg

E

4M

10kg

A: Pendulum A
B: Pendulum B
C: Pendulum C
D: Pendulum D
E: Pendulum E

20) The mass below is displaced from a point level with X. Which of the following graphs represents the motion of the mass in relation to its starting point, after being released?

100g < X

A Displacement / Time
B Displacement / Time
C Displacement / Time
D Displacement / Time
E Displacement / Time

A: Graph A
B: Graph B
C: Graph C
D: Graph D
E: Graph E

Chapter 9

Answers

Verbal reasoning — synonyms

Page Number	Question Number	Answer
13	1	E

Of the five options the word which comes closest in meaning to *complacency* is *smugness* – option E.

Page Number	Question Number	Answer
14	2	A

Of the five options the word which comes closest in meaning to *ascetic* is *austere* – option A.

The correct answers for the remainder of the synonyms section are as follows:

Page Number	Question Number	Answer
14	3	B
14	4	C
14	5	B
14	6	E
15	7	B
15	8	B
15	9	D
15	10	E

Verbal reasoning — analogies

Page Number	Question Number	Answer
16	11	D

The relationship between *spider* and *web* is simply that a web is the official name for a spider's home. Similarly, a *warren* is the official name for a *rabbit's* home.

Page Number	Question Number	Answer
16	12	A

The relationship between *book* and *library* is simply that a library describes a large collection of books. Similarly, a *gallery* describes a large collection of *paintings*.

The correct answers for the remainder of the analogies section are as follows:

Page Number	Question Number	Answer
16	13	D
16	14	B
16	15	B
16	16	D
17	17	C
17	18	B
17	19	B
17	20	A
17	21	C
17	22	B
17	23	C
17	24	B
18	25	B
18	26	C
18	27	D
18	28	C
18	29	C
18	30	C

Verbal reasoning — antonyms

Page Number	Question Number	Answer
18	31	A

Of the five multiple-choice options the one which comes closest to the opposite of *mean* is *generous* – option A.

Page Number	Question Number	Answer
19	32	B

Of the five multiple-choice options the one which comes closest to the opposite of *sincere* is *hypocritical* – option B.

The correct answers for the remainder of the antonyms section are as follows:

Page Number	Question Number	Answer
19	33	C
19	34	D
19	35	E
19	36	A
19	37	B
19	38	C
19	39	D
19	40	E

Verbal reasoning — word groups

Page Number	Question Number	Answer
19	41	D

The common connection between the following four multiple-choice options is that they are all colours: *turquoise; cyan; cerise;* and *magenta*. The odd one out is therefore the fifth multiple-choice option, which is *turpentine* – option D.

Page Number	Question Number	Answer
20	42	E

The common connection between the following four multiple-choice options is that they are all types of fish: *sole; haddock; salmon;* and *trout*. The odd one out is therefore the fifth multiple-choice option, which is *frog* – option E.

The correct answers for the remainder of the word groups section are as follows:

Page Number	Question Number	Answer
20	43	C
20	44	E
20	45	C
20	46	B
20	47	B
20	48	A
20	49	D
20	50	B

Verbal reasoning — comprehension

Page Number	Question Number	Answer
22	51	A

The section of the text which provides the answer to question 51 is as follows:
'... *John Ruskin, the eminent Victorian art critic ...*'
The statement '*John Ruskin was a more important art critic than Charles Dickens*' is therefore correct – option A.

Page Number	Question Number	Answer
22	52	B

The section of the text which provides the answer to question 52 is as follows:
'...*Their paintings often featured religious, mythical or symbolic subjects. Paying meticulous attention to detail and striving for truth in art, the Pre-Raphaelites painted directly from nature and used ordinary people as their models. ...*'
The statement '*The Pre-Raphaelites were concerned with realism and honesty, wanting to depict ordinary people*' is therefore incorrect – option B.

The correct answers for the remainder of the comprehension section are as follows:

Page Number	Question Number	Answer
22	53	A
22	54	A
22	55	A
22	56	B
23	57	B
23	58	A
23	59	B
23	60	B
23	61	A
24	62	B
24	63	A
24	64	A
24	65	B

Numerical reasoning — number series

Page Number	Question Number	Answer
25	1	A

The numbers from question 1 are shown in bold print in the mathematical explanation below. There are two mathematical operations at each stage of this series. The first is division by 2 and the second is to subtract 8.

1664 / 2 = 832   832 – 8 = 824

824 / 2 = 412   412 – 8 = 404

404 / 2 = 202   202 – 8 = 194

194 / 2 = 97   97 – 8 = **?**

The correct answer is therefore **89** – option A.

Page Number	Question Number	Answer
25	2	C

The numerical series proceeds in increasing multiples.

3 x 3 = 9

9 x 4 = 36

36 x 5 = **?**

? x 6 = 1080

The correct answer is therefore **180** – option C. As you can see, the answer could have been worked out by multiplying 36 by 5 or by dividing 1080 by 6.

The correct answers for the remainder of the number series section are as follows:

Page Number	Question Number	Answer
25	3	B
26	4	E
26	5	A
26	6	D
26	7	A

Page Number	Question Number	Answer
26	8	A
26	9	A
26	10	C
26	11	C
26	12	C
27	13	D
27	14	D
27	15	E
27	16	A
27	17	D
27	18	E
27	19	B
27	20	B
27	21	C
28	22	D
28	23	E
28	24	E
28	25	D
28	26	E
28	27	C
28	28	C
28	29	C
28	30	A

Numerical reasoning (in context)

Page Number	Question Number	Answer
29	31	B

The 8% compound interest rate in the table shows that £100.00 after five years earns £46.93 in interest. The total compound interest on £200.00 at a rate of 8% over five years will be twice this amount, so

$$2 \times £46.93 = £93.86$$

The correct answer is therefore option B.

Page Number	Question Number	Answer
29	32	C

The 9% compound interest rate in the table shows that £100.00 after five years earns £53.86 in interest. The total compound interest on £300.00 at a rate of 9% over five years will be three times this amount, so

$$3 \times £53.86 = £161.58$$

The total compound interest on £300.00 at a rate of 9% over five years will be three times this amount, so

$$3 \times £45.00 = £135.00$$

The difference between the compound and simple interest earned is

$$£161.58 - £135.00 = £26.58$$

The correct answer is therefore option C.

Page Number	Question Number	Answer
29	33	D

The 7% and 9% compound interest rates after five years are shown in the table as £40.26 and £53.86 respectively.

The total compound interest on £200.00 after five years at 7% is therefore twice this amount

$$2 \times £40.26 = £80.52$$

The total compound interest on £200.00 after five years at 9% is therefore twice £53.86

$$2 \times £53.86 = £107.72$$

The difference between these two amounts is

$$£107.72 - £80.52 = £27.20$$

The correct answer is therefore option D.

The correct answers for the remainder of the numerical reasoning (in context) section are as follows:

Page Number	Question Number	Answer
30	34	B
30	35	C
30	36	A
31	37	C
31	38	A
31	39	E
32	40	A
32	41	C
32	42	B
33	43	B
33	44	E
33	45	A
34	46	C
34	47	A
34	48	B
35	49	B
35	50	D
35	51	C
36	52	A
36	53	D
36	54	C
37	55	D
37	56	A
37	57	E
38	58	D
38	59	E
38	60	B

Clerical

Page Number	Question Number	Answer
39	1	pessimistic, systematically, alleviate, excruciating, patience

The correct spellings for those words which have been misspelt are as follows:

pessimistic, systematically, alleviate, excruciating, patience

Page Number	Question Number	Answer
39	2	professor, confidential, fourteenth, February

The correct spellings for those words which have been misspelt are as follows:

professor, confidential, fourteenth, February

The correct answers for the remainder of the clerical section are as follows:

Page Number	Question Number	Answer
39	3	autumn, residents, neighbouring, vehicles
40	4	world, participants, spanning
40	5	millennium, torrential, devastated
40	6	ferocious, prey, leopard, stealthily
40	7	proficiency, advisable
40	8	stationery, precaution, straight
40	9	cumulative, density, parameters
40	10	conservationists, desperate, specialise, debris
40	11	wholeheartedly, committee
40	12	pungent, poisonous, pesticides, itchy
40	13	disillusioned, performance
40	14	gymnasium, equipment, recommended
41	15	jewellery, occasion, visible, gaily, rhythm
41	16	chimney-pot, mantelpiece, financially
41	17	misspell, illegible
41	18	perishable, delicatessen, separately
41	19	endurance, potential, forecast
41	20	apartment, accumulated

Non-verbal reasoning

Page Number	Question Number	Answer
43	1	C

The shape in the top left of the 2 by 2 cell is a small white circle and the shape in the top right of the 4 by 4 cell is a small black circle. The shape in the bottom left of the 2 by 2 cell is a large white circle. The shape which is most appropriate for the bottom right of the 2 by 2 cell is therefore a large black circle.

The answer to question 1 could therefore be either A or C.

The curved line across the top left of the 2 by 2 cell is reflected in the cell on the top right. The curved line in the cell on the bottom left therefore needs to be reflected in the bottom right.

The correct answer to question 1 is therefore C.

Page Number	Question Number	Answer
43	2	D

The shapes in the left-hand column of the 3 by 3 cell have each been rotated by 45 degrees in the middle column. The shapes in the middle column of the 3 by 3 cell have similarly been rotated by 45 degrees – to give the shapes in the right-hand column. In terms of the missing central cell it therefore needs to be the same as the left-hand cell when it has been rotated by 45 degrees.

·The correct answer is therefore D.

The correct answers for the remainder of the non-verbal reasoning section are as follows:

Page Number	Question Number	Answer
43	3	E
43	4	A
44	5	E
44	6	C
44	7	A
44	8	B
45	9	C
45	10	E
45	11	A
45	12	B
46	13	B
46	14	C
46	15	D
46	16	B
47	17	D
47	18	C
47	19	B
47	20	A

Mechanical reasoning

Page Number	Question Number	Answer
49	1	C

The crowbar with the longest handle makes lifting the load the easiest. The correct answer is therefore C.

Page Number	Question Number	Answer
49	2	E

The person who exerts the least pressure on the platform is dependent upon the person's weight and also the size of their feet (i.e. the area of contact between their feet and the platform). The lightest weight of the five people shown is 55kg, so the answer is either A or E – both of which weigh 55kg. Since E has larger feet than A the correct answer is E.

The correct answers for the remainder of the mechanical reasoning section are as follows:

Page Number	Question Number	Answer
49	3	C
49	4	D
50	5	A
50	6	D
50	7	A
50	8	B
51	9	E
51	10	C
51	11	A
51	12	D
52	13	D
52	14	A
52	15	D
52	16	B
53	17	E
53	18	D
53	19	B
53	20	A